60
SUMMERTIME
FAMILY
devotions

The quoted ideas expressed in this book (but not Scripture verses) are not, in all cases, exact quotations, as some have been edited for clarity and brevity. In all cases, the author has attempted to maintain the speaker's original intent. In some cases, quoted material for this book was obtained from secondary sources, primarily print media. While every effort was made to ensure the accuracy of these sources, the accuracy cannot be guaranteed. For additions, deletions, corrections, or clarifications in future editions of this text, please write Freeman-Smith, LLC.

The Holy Bible, King James Version

The Holy Bible, New King James Version (NKJV) Copyright © 1982 by Thomas Nelson, Inc. Used by permission.

The Holy Bible. New Living Translation (NLT) copyright © 1996 Tyndale Charitable Trust. Used by permission of Tyndale House Publishers.

Scripture taken from The Message. (MSG) Copyright © 1993, 1994, 1995, 1996, 2000, 2001, 2002. Used by permission of NavPress Publishing Group.

The Holman Christian Standard Bible™ (Holman CSB) Copyright © 1999, 2000, 2001 by Holman Bible Publishers. Used by permission.

Cover Design by Kim Russell / Wahoo Designs
Page Layout by Bart Dawson

ISBN 978-1-60587-069-4

Printed in the United States of America

60 SUMMERTIME FAMILY devotions

INTRODUCTION

Choose for yourselves this day whom you will serve . . . .
But as for me and my house, we will serve the Lord.

Joshua 24:15 NKJV

How can you make this the best summer ever?
By spending it with God. And the ideas in
this devotional book can help.

This text contains 60 daily devotionals for your
family to read together this summer. The ideas
on these pages are common-sense tools that can
help you build your family's collective life upon
the only foundation that can never be shaken—the
foundation of God's Holy Word. God's promises
are found in a book like no other: the Holy Bible.

As you prepare for the summer ahead—and
as you prepare for the ups, the downs, and the
complications of life here in the 21st century—you
should arm yourself with the promises and
principles found in God's Word. When you do,
then you and your loved ones can expect the best,
not only for the day ahead or for the summer ahead,
but also for all eternity.

MAKING THIS THE
BEST SUMMER EVER

Rejoice in the Lord always. I will say it again: Rejoice!
Philippians 4:4 Holman CSB

The 118th Psalm reminds us that today, like every other day, is a cause for celebration. God gives us this day. He fills it to the brim with possibilities, and He challenges us to use it for His purposes. The day is presented to us fresh and clean at midnight, free of charge, but we must beware: Each day is a non-renewable resource—once it's gone, it's gone forever. Our responsibility, of course, is to use this day in the service of God's will and according to His commandments.

If you want to make this the best summer ever, celebrate it as a gift from God. Treasure the time that God has given you, and while you're at it, give God the praise that He deserves. Search for the hidden possibilities that God has placed along your paths. This summer season is a priceless gift from God; use it joyfully and encourage others to do likewise.

MORE THOUGHTS ABOUT CELEBRATING LIFE

Our sense of joy, satisfaction, and fulfillment in life increases, no matter what the circumstances, if we are in the center of God's will.

Billy Graham

If you can forgive the person you were, accept the person you are, and believe in the person you will become, you are headed for joy. So celebrate your life.

Barbara Johnson

Unparalleled joy and victory come from allowing Christ to do "the hard thing" with us.

Beth Moore

Joy is the direct result of having God's perspective on our daily lives and the effect of loving our Lord enough to obey His commands and trust His promises.

Bill Bright

A life of intimacy with God is characterized by joy.

Oswald Chambers

Words fail to express my love for this Holy Book, my gratitude for its author, for His love and goodness. How shall I thank Him for it?

Lottie Moon

A SUMMERTIME TIP

Every day this summer should be a cause for celebration. God has given you the gift of life (here on earth) and the promise of eternal life (in heaven). Now, He wants you to celebrate those gifts.

CARING FOR YOUR
FAMILY THIS SUMMER

*Now if anyone does not provide for his own relatives,
and especially for his household, he has denied
the faith and is worse than an unbeliever.*
1 Timothy 5:8 Holman CSB

In a world filled with countless obligations and frequent frustrations, we may be tempted to take our families for granted. But God intends otherwise.

Our families are precious gifts from our Father in heaven. If we are to be the righteous men and women that God intends, we must care for our families, we must love our families, we must lead our families, and we must make time for our families, even when the demands of the day are great.

No family is perfect, and neither is yours. But, despite the inevitable challenges, obligations, and hurt feelings of family life, your clan is God's blessing to you. That little band of men, women, kids, and babies is a priceless treasure on temporary loan from the Father above. Give thanks to the Giver for the gift of family . . . and act accordingly.

More Thoughts About Family

It is a reverent thing to see an ancient castle or building not in decay, or to see a fair timber tree sound and perfect. How much more beautiful it is to behold an ancient and noble family that has stood against the waves and weathers of time.

Francis Bacon

Never give your family the leftovers and crumbs of your time.

Charles Swindoll

The only true source of meaning in life is found in love for God and His son Jesus Christ, and love for mankind, beginning with our own families.

James Dobson

A home is a place where we find direction.

Gigi Graham Tchividjian

When you think about it for a moment, it certainly makes sense that if people can establish a loving and compatible relationship at home, they have a better chance of establishing winning relationships with those with whom they work on a regular basis.

Zig Ziglar

Living life with a consistent spiritual walk deeply influences those we love most.

Vonette Bright

A SUMMERTIME TIP

Think safety: the summer is a fun time, but it can also be a dangerous time. So whether you're at the beach, at the lake, in the woods, or anyplace in between, think about safety first and having fun next.

3

SPENDING EVERY DAY
THROUGHOUT THE
SUMMER WITH GOD

He awakens [Me] each morning; He awakens
My ear to listen like those being instructed.
The Lord God has opened My ear,
and I was not rebellious; I did not turn back.

Isaiah 50:4-5 Holman CSB

E ach new day is a gift from God, and if we are
wise, we spend a few quiet moments each
morning thanking the Giver. Daily life is
woven together with the threads of habit, and no
habit is more important to our spiritual health than
the discipline of daily prayer and devotion to the
Creator.

When we begin each day with heads bowed and
hearts lifted, we remind ourselves of God's love,
His protection, and His commandments. And if we
are wise, we align our priorities for the coming day
with the teachings and commandments that God
has given us through His Holy Word.

So, today, and every day this summer, and every day after that, ask for God's help and ask for it often . . . starting with your morning devotional.

MORE THOUGHTS ABOUT YOUR DAILY DEVOTIONAL

God is a place of safety you can run to, but it helps if you are running to Him on a daily basis so that you are in familiar territory.

Stormie Omartian

If you, too, will learn to wait upon God, to get alone with Him, and remain silent so that you can hear His voice when He is ready to speak to you, what a difference it will make in your life!

Kay Arthur

Make a plan now to keep a daily appointment with God. The enemy is going to tell you to set it aside, but you must carve out the time. If you're too busy to meet with the Lord, friend, then you are simply too busy.

Charles Swindoll

What digestion is to the body, meditation is to the soul.

Warren Wiersbe

How motivating it has been for me to view my early morning devotions as time of retreat alone with Jesus, who desires that I "come with Him by myself to a quiet place" in order to pray, read His Word, listen for His voice, and be renewed in my spirit.

Anne Graham Lotz

A SUMMERTIME TIP

If you're wise, you'll place a high priority this summer on the quiet time you spend with God each day. If you can't find time for God, then it's time to give your "to-do" list a major overhaul.

FOLLOWING JESUS
TODAY AND EVERY DAY

The one who loves his life will lose it, and the one who
hates his life in this world will keep it for eternal life.
If anyone serves Me, he must follow Me.
Where I am, there My servant also will be.
If anyone serves Me, the Father will honor him.
John 12:25-26 Holman CSB

I f you want to make this a memorable summer, spend it following Jesus.

Jesus walks with every member of your family. Are you walking with Him? Hopefully, all of you will choose to walk with Him today and every day of your lives. And hopefully, you will encourage others to do the same.

God's Word is clear: When we genuinely invite Christ to reign over our hearts, and when we accept His transforming love, we are forever changed. When we welcome Christ into our hearts, an old life ends and a new way of living—along with a completely new way of viewing the world—begins.

Each morning offers a fresh opportunity to invite Christ, yet once again, to rule over our hearts and our days. Each morning presents yet another opportunity to take up His cross and follow in His footsteps. Today, let us rejoice in the new life that is ours through Christ, and let us follow Him, step by step, on the path that He first walked.

MORE THOUGHTS ABOUT FOLLOWING CHRIST

A believer comes to Christ; a disciple follows after Him.

Vance Havner

Christ is not valued at all unless He is valued above all.

St. Augustine

It's your heart that Jesus longs for: your will to be made His own with self on the cross forever, and Jesus alone on the throne.

Ruth Bell Graham

Jesus challenges you and me to keep our focus daily on the cross of His will if we want to be His disciples.

Anne Graham Lotz

The Christian faith is meant to be lived moment by moment. It isn't some broad, general outline—it's a long walk with a real Person. Details count: passing thoughts, small sacrifices, a few encouraging words, little acts of kindness, brief victories over nagging sins.

Joni Eareckson Tada

SOMETHING TO THINK ABOUT

Jesus made an extreme sacrifice for you. What kind of sacrifice are you willing to make for Him?

KEEPING THE RIGHT KIND OF ATTITUDE THROUGHOUT THE SUMMER

For God has not given us a spirit of fearfulness,
but one of power, love, and sound judgment.
2 Timothy 1:7 Holman CSB

The Christian life is a cause for celebration, but sometimes we don't feel much like celebrating. In fact, when the weight of the world bears down upon our shoulders, celebration may be the last thing on our minds . . . but it shouldn't be. As God's children—and as the parents and grandparents of our own clan—we have been blessed beyond measure.

Remember this: today is a non-renewable resource—once it's gone, it's gone forever. So this summer, and every season hereafter, celebrate the life that God has given you by thinking optimistically about your family and your future. Give thanks to the One who has showered you with blessings, and trust in your heart that He wants to give you so much more.

MORE THOUGHTS ABOUT ATTITUDE

Life is 10% what happens to you and 90% how you respond to it.

Charles Swindoll

Attitude is all-important. Let the soul take a quiet attitude of faith and love toward God, and from there on, the responsibility is God's. He will make good on His commitments.

A. W. Tozer

Attitude is the mind's paintbrush; it can color any situation.

Barbara Johnson

I could go through this day oblivious to the miracles all around me, or I could tune in and "enjoy."

Gloria Gaither

The things we think are the things that feed our souls. If we think on pure and lovely things, we shall grow pure and lovely like them; and the converse is equally true.

Hannah Whitall Smith

I became aware of one very important concept I had missed before: my attitude—not my circumstances—was what was making me unhappy.

Vonette Bright

SOMETHING TO THINK ABOUT

Attitudes are contagious, so it's important to make your home a haven of optimism, encouragement, and hope.

TRUSTING GOD'S PROMISES THROUGHOUT THE SUMMER AND BEYOND

For you need endurance, so that after you have done God's will, you may receive what was promised.

Hebrews 10:36 Holman CSB

The Bible contains promises, made by God, upon which we, as believers, can and must depend. But sometimes, especially when we find ourselves caught in the inevitable entanglements of life, we fail to trust God completely.

Are you tired? Discouraged? Fearful? Be comforted and trust the promises that God has made to you. Are you worried or anxious? Be confident in God's power. Do you see a difficult future ahead? Be courageous and call upon God. He will protect you and then use you according to His purposes. Are you confused? Listen to the quiet voice of your Heavenly Father. He is not a God of confusion. Talk with Him; listen to Him; trust Him, and trust His promises. He is steadfast, and He is your Protector . . . forever.

MORE THOUGHTS ABOUT GOD'S PROMISES

Shake the dust from your past, and move forward in His promises.

Kay Arthur

God does not give us everything we want, but He does fulfill all His promises as He leads us along the best and straightest paths to Himself.

Dietrich Bonhoeffer

Claim all of God's promises in the Bible. Your sins, your worries, your life—you may cast them all on Him.

Corrie ten Boom

We can have full confidence in God's promises because we can have full faith in His character.

Franklin Graham

We honor God by asking for great things when they are a part of His promise. We dishonor Him and cheat ourselves when we ask for molehills where He has promised mountains.

Vance Havner

God's promises are medicine for the broken heart. Let Him comfort you. And, after He has comforted you, try to share that comfort with somebody else. It will do both of you good.

Warren Wiersbe

SOMETHING TO THINK ABOUT

God will most certainly keep His promises to you. Your job is to keep your obligations to Him.

HAVING FUN THIS SUMMER

Young man, it's wonderful to be young! Enjoy every minute of it. Do everything you want to do; take it all in. But remember that you must give an account to God for everything you do.

Ecclesiastes 11:9 NLT

Are you a family who takes time each day to really enjoy life? And are you determined to have fun this summer? Hopefully so. After all, God has seen fit to give you the gift of life. So it is incumbent upon you to use it and to enjoy it. But sometimes, amid the inevitable pressures of everyday living, really enjoying life may seem almost impossible. It is not.

For most of us, fun is as much a function of attitude as it is a function of environment. So whether you're standing victorious atop one of life's mountains or trudging through one of life's valleys, enjoy yourself. You deserve to have fun today, and God wants you to have fun today . . . so what on earth are you waiting for?

MORE THOUGHTS ABOUT HAVING FUN

Our thoughts, not our circumstances, determine our happiness.

John Maxwell

Whence comes this idea that if what we are doing is fun, it can't be God's will? The God who made giraffes, a baby's fingernails, a puppy's tail, a crooknecked squash, the bobwhite's call, and a young girl's giggle, has a sense of humor. Make no mistake about that.

Catherine Marshall

A SUMMERTIME TIP

Summertime can be fun-time, and it should be. But every season is the right time to honor God with your thoughts, your actions, and your prayers.

LISTENING TO YOUR CONSCIENCE

*Now the goal of our instruction is love from
a pure heart, a good conscience, and a sincere faith.*
1 Timothy 1:5 Holman CSB

If you want to have a happy, healthy summer, listen carefully to your conscience. Very carefully.

Billy Graham correctly observed, "Most of us follow our conscience as we follow a wheelbarrow. We push it in front of us in the direction we want to go." To do so, of course, is a profound mistake. Yet all of us, on occasion, have failed to listen to the voice that God planted in our hearts, and all of us have suffered the consequences.

God gave you a conscience for a very good reason: to make your path conform to His will. Wise believers make it a practice to listen carefully to that quiet internal voice. Count yourself among that number. When your conscience speaks, listen and learn. In all likelihood, God is trying to get His message through. And in all likelihood, it is a message that you desperately need to hear.

26

MORE THOUGHTS ABOUT
LISTENING TO YOUR CONSCIENCE

To go against one's conscience is neither safe nor right. Here I stand. I cannot do otherwise.

Martin Luther

The convicting work of the Holy Spirit awakens, disturbs, and judges.

Franklin Graham

Your conscience is your alarm system. It's your protection.

Charles Stanley

The voice of the subconscious argues with you, tries to convince you; but the inner voice of God does not argue; it does not try to convince you. It just speaks, and it is self-authenticating.

E. Stanley Jones

God desires that we become spiritually healthy enough through faith to have a conscience that rightly interprets the work of the Holy Spirit.

Beth Moore

There is a difficulty about disagreeing with God. He is the source from which all your reasoning power comes: you could not be right and He wrong any more than a stream can rise higher than its own source. When you are arguing against Him you are arguing against the very power that makes you able to argue at all: it is like cutting off the branch you are sitting on.

C. S. Lewis

REMEMBER THIS

God gave you a conscience for a very good reason: to use it.

LIVING COURAGEOUSLY
THIS SUMMER

The Lord is the One who will go before you.
He will be with you; He will not leave you or
forsake you. Do not be afraid or discouraged.

Deuteronomy 31:8 Holman CSB

Christians have every reason to live courageously. After all, the ultimate battle has already been fought and won on the cross at Calvary. But, even dedicated followers of Christ may find their courage tested by the inevitable disappointments and tragedies that occur in the lives of believers and non-believers alike.

Every human life is a tapestry of events: some wonderful, some not-so-wonderful, and some downright disheartening. When the storm clouds form overhead and we find ourselves wandering through the dark valley of despair, our faith is stretched, sometimes to the breaking point. But as believers, we can be comforted: Wherever we find ourselves, whether at the top of the mountain or the depths of the valley, God is there, and because He cares for us, we can live courageously.

The next time you find yourself in a fear-provoking situation, remember that God is as near as your next breath, and remember that He offers salvation to His children. He is your shield and your strength; He is your protector and your deliverer. Call upon Him in your hour of need and then be comforted. Whatever your challenge, whatever your trouble, God can handle it. And will.

MORE THOUGHTS ABOUT COURAGE

What is courage? It is the ability to be strong in trust, in conviction, in obedience. To be courageous is to step out in faith—to trust and obey, no matter what.

Kay Arthur

If a person fears God, he or she has no reason to fear anything else. On the other hand, if a person does not fear God, then fear becomes a way of life.

Beth Moore

When once we are assured that God is good, then there can be nothing left to fear.

Hannah Whitall Smith

Jesus Christ can make the weakest man into a divine dreadnought, fearing nothing.

Oswald Chambers

Take courage. We walk in the wilderness today and in the Promised Land tomorrow.

D. L. Moody

SOMETHING TO THINK ABOUT

If you trust God completely and without reservation, you have every reason on earth—and in heaven—to live courageously. And that's precisely what you should do.

10

COUNTING YOUR BLESSINGS ALL SUMMER LONG

I will make them and the area around My hill
a blessing: I will send down showers in their season—
showers of blessing.

Ezekiel 34:26 Holman CSB

If you sat down and began counting your blessings, how long would it take? A very, very long time! Your blessings include life, freedom, family, friends, talents, and possessions, for starters. But, your greatest blessing—a gift that is yours for the asking—is God's gift of salvation through Christ Jesus.

Today, begin making a list of your blessings. You most certainly will not be able to make a complete list, but take a few moments and jot down as many blessings as you can. Then give thanks to the giver of all good things: God. His love for you is eternal, as are His gifts. And it's never too soon—or too late—to offer Him thanks.

MORE THOUGHTS ABOUT
GOD'S BLESSINGS

Do we not continually pass by blessings innumerable without notice, and instead fix our eyes on what we feel to be our trials and our losses, and think and talk about these until our whole horizon is filled with them, and we almost begin to think we have no blessings at all?

Hannah Whitall Smith

Think of the blessings we so easily take for granted: Life itself; preservation from danger; every bit of health we enjoy; every hour of liberty; the ability to see, to hear, to speak, to think, and to imagine all this comes from the hand of God.

Billy Graham

When you and I are related to Jesus Christ, our strength and wisdom and peace and joy and love and hope may run out, but His life rushes in to keep us filled to the brim. We are showered with blessings, not because of anything we have or have not done, but simply because of Him.

Anne Graham Lotz

Jesus intended for us to be overwhelmed by the blessings of regular days. He said it was the reason He had come: "I am come that they might have life, and that they might have it more abundantly."

Gloria Gaither

God's kindness is not like the sunset—brilliant in its intensity, but dying every second. God's generosity keeps coming and coming and coming.

Bill Hybels

SOMETHING TO THINK ABOUT

God gives us countless blessings. We, in turn, should give Him our thanks and our praise.

DREAMING BIG DREAMS THIS SUMMER

Now glory be to God! By his mighty power at work within us, he is able to accomplish infinitely more than we would ever dare to ask or hope.

Ephesians 3:20 NLT

A re you willing to entertain the possibility that God has big plans in store for your family? Hopefully so. Yet sometimes, especially if you've recently experienced a life-altering disappointment, you may find it difficult to envision a brighter future for yourself and your family. If so, it's time to reconsider your own capabilities . . . and God's.

Your Heavenly Father created you with unique gifts and untapped talents; your job is to tap them. When you do, you'll begin to feel an increasing sense of confidence in yourself and in your future.

It takes courage to dream big dreams. You will discover that courage when you do three things: accept the past, trust God to handle the future, and make the most of the time He has given you today.

MORE THOUGHTS ABOUT DREAMS

The future lies all before us. Shall it only be a slight advance upon what we usually do? Ought it not to be a bound, a leap forward to altitudes of endeavor and success undreamed of before?

Annie Armstrong

Allow your dreams a place in your prayers and plans. God-given dreams can help you move into the future He is preparing for you.

Barbara Johnson

REMEMBER THIS

You can dream big dreams, but you can never out-dream God. His plans for you are even bigger than you can imagine.

ENTHUSED ABOUT
THE SUMMER,
ENTHUSED ABOUT LIFE

Whatever you do, do it enthusiastically,
as something done for the Lord and not for men.

Colossians 3:23 Holman CSB

D o you see this summer season, and every season after that, as a glorious opportunity to serve God and to do His will? Are you enthused about life, or do you struggle through each day giving scarcely a thought to God's blessings? Are you constantly praising God for His gifts, and are you sharing His Good News with the world? And are you excited about the possibilities for service that God has placed before you, whether at home, at work, at church? You should be.

You are the recipient of Christ's sacrificial love. Accept it enthusiastically and share it fervently. Jesus deserves your enthusiasm; the world deserves it; and you deserve the experience of sharing it.

MORE THOUGHTS ABOUT ENTHUSIASM

Enthusiasm, like the flu, is contagious—we get it from one another.

Barbara Johnson

One of the great needs in the church today is for every Christian to become enthusiastic about his faith in Jesus Christ.

Billy Graham

A SUMMERTIME TIP

Make this summer a time of great enthusiasm for your life and your faith. When you become genuinely enthused about your life and your faith, you'll guard your heart and improve your life.

MAKING WISE CHOICES

I have set before you life and death, blessing and curse.
Choose life so that you and your descendants may live,
love the Lord your God, obey Him, and remain faithful
to Him. For He is your life, and He will prolong
your life in the land the Lord swore to give to your
fathers Abraham, Isaac, and Jacob.
Deuteronomy 30:19-20 Holman CSB

If you want to enjoy a healthy, enjoyable, productive summer, then you should start by making wise choices. Life is a series of choices. Each day, we make countless decisions that can bring us closer to God . . . or not. When we live according to God's commandments, we earn for ourselves the abundance and peace that He intends for our lives. But, when we turn our backs upon God by disobeying Him, we bring needless suffering upon ourselves and our families.

Do you seek spiritual abundance that can be yours through the person of God's only begotten Son? Then invite Christ into your heart and live according to His teachings. And, when you confront a difficult decision or a powerful temptation, seek God's wisdom and trust it. When you do, you will receive untold blessings—not only for this day, but also for all eternity.

MORE THOUGHTS ABOUT THE IMPORTANCE OF MAKING WISE CHOICES

Life is a series of choices between the bad, the good, and the best. Everything depends on how we choose.

Vance Havner

Freedom is not the right to do what we want but the power to do what we ought.

Corrie ten Boom

Every day, I find countless opportunities to decide whether I will obey God and demonstrate my love for Him or try to please myself or the world system. God is waiting for my choices.

Bill Bright

We are either the masters or the victims of our attitudes. It is a matter of personal choice. Who we are today is the result of choices we made yesterday. Tomorrow, we will become what we choose today. To change means to choose to change.

John Maxwell

SOMETHING TO THINK ABOUT

Little decisions, when taken together over a long period of time, can have big consequences. So remember that when it comes to matters of health, fitness, stress, and spirituality, there are no small decisions.

14

TRUST HIM

*Trust in the Lord with all your heart, and do not rely
on your own understanding; think about Him
in all your ways, and He will guide you
on the right paths.*

Proverbs 3:5-6 Holman CSB

Sometimes the future seems bright, and sometimes it does not. Yet even when we cannot see the possibilities of tomorrow, God can. As believers, our challenge is to trust an uncertain future to an all-powerful God.

When we trust God, we should trust Him without reservation. We should steel ourselves against the inevitable disappointments of the day, secure in the knowledge that our Heavenly Father has a plan for the future that only He can see.

Can you place your future into the hands of a loving and all-knowing God? Can you live amid the uncertainties of today, knowing that God has dominion over all your tomorrows? If you can, you are wise and you are blessed. When you trust God with everything you are and everything you have, He will bless you now and forever.

MORE THOUGHTS ABOUT TRUSTING GOD

Do not be afraid, then, that if you trust, or tell others to trust, the matter will end there. Trust is only the beginning and the continual foundation. When we trust Him, the Lord works, and His work is the important part of the whole matter.

Hannah Whitall Smith

Brother, is your faith looking upward today? / Trust in the promise of the Savior. / Sister, is the light shining bright on your way? / Trust in the promise of thy Lord.

Fanny Crosby

Sometimes the very essence of faith is trusting God in the midst of things He knows good and well we cannot comprehend.

Beth Moore

Are you serious about wanting God's guidance to become the person He wants you to be? The first step is to tell God that you know you can't manage your own life; that you need His help.

Catherine Marshall

As God's children, we are the recipients of lavish love—a love that motivates us to keep trusting even when we have no idea what God is doing.

Beth Moore

REMEMBER THIS

Because God is trustworthy—and because He has made promises to you that He intends to keep—you are protected.

SETTING THE RIGHT
KIND OF EXAMPLE
THIS SUMMER

Set an example of good works yourself,
with integrity and dignity in your teaching.
Titus 2:7 Holman CSB

Whether we like it or not, all of us are role models. Our friends and family members watch our actions and, as followers of Christ, we are obliged to act accordingly.

What kind of example is your family? Does your clan serve as a genuine example of righteousness? Are you positive role models for others? Are you the kind of people whose actions, day in and day out, are based upon kindness, faithfulness, and a love for the Lord? If so, you are not only blessed by God, but you are also a powerful force for good in a world that desperately needs positive influences such as yours.

Corrie ten Boom advised, "Don't worry about what you do not understand. Worry about what you do understand in the Bible but do not live by." And that's sound advice because our family members and friends are watching . . . and so, for that matter, is God.

MORE THOUGHTS ABOUT SETTING THE RIGHT KIND OF EXAMPLE

There is a transcendent power in example. We reform others unconsciously when we walk uprightly.

Anne Sophie Swetchine

REMEMBER THIS

God wants you to be positive role models. And that's what you should want, too.

THE POWER OF FAITH

Now faith is the reality of what is hoped for,
the proof of what is not seen.

Hebrews 11:1 Holman CSB

The first element of a successful summer (and the first elelent of a successful life) is faith: faith in God, faith in His Son, and faith in His promises. If we place our lives in God's hands, our faith is rewarded in ways that we—as human beings with clouded vision and limited understanding—can scarcely comprehend. But, if we seek to rely solely upon our own resources, or if we seek earthly success outside the boundaries of God's commandments, we reap a bitter harvest for ourselves and for our loved ones.

Do you desire the abundance and success that God has promised? Then trust Him today and every day that you live. Trust Him with every aspect of your life. Trust His promises, and trust in the saving grace of His only begotten Son. Then, when you have entrusted your future to the Giver of all things good, rest assured that your future is secure, not only for today, but also for all eternity.

MORE THOUGHTS ABOUT FAITH

Faith does not concern itself with the entire journey. One step is enough.

Mrs. Charles E. Cowman

Just as our faith strengthens our prayer life, so do our prayers deepen our faith. Let us pray often, starting today, for a deeper, more powerful faith.

Shirley Dobson

There are a lot of things in life that are difficult to understand. Faith allows the soul to go beyond what the eyes can see.

John Maxwell

When you enroll in the "school of faith," you never know what may happen next. The life of faith presents challenges that keep you going—and keep you growing!

Warren Wiersbe

Nothing is more disastrous than to study faith, analyze faith, make noble resolves of faith, but never actually to make the leap of faith.

Vance Havner

If God chooses to remain silent, faith is content.

Ruth Bell Graham

REMEMBER THIS

If your faith is strong enough, you and God—working together—can move mountains.

A Spiritual Journey Throughout the Summer . . . and Beyond

But grow in the grace and knowledge of our Lord and Savior Jesus Christ. To Him be the glory both now and to the day of eternity.

2 Peter 3:18 Holman CSB

The journey toward spiritual maturity cannot be completed in a single season; it's a journey that lasts a lifetime: As Christians, we can and should continue to grow in the love and the knowledge of our Savior as long as we live. When we cease to grow, either emotionally or spiritually, we do ourselves and our loved ones a profound disservice. But, if we study God's Word, if we obey His commandments, and if we live in the center of His will, we will not be "stagnant" believers; we will, instead, be growing Christians . . . and that's exactly what God wants for our lives.

We must seek to grow in our knowledge and love of the Lord every day that we live. In those quiet moments when we open our hearts to God, the One who made us keeps remaking us. He gives us direction, perspective, wisdom, and courage. The appropriate moment to accept those spiritual gifts is the present one.

MORE THOUGHTS ABOUT SPIRITUAL GROWTH

God does not discipline us to subdue us, but to condition us for a life of usefulness and blessedness.

Billy Graham

Our Heavenly Father knows to place us where we may learn lessons impossible anywhere else. He has neither misplaced nor displaced us.

Elisabeth Elliot

Kindness in this world will do much to help others, not only to come into the light, but also to grow in grace day by day.

Fanny Crosby

We have tasted "that the Lord is good" (Psalm 34:8), but we don't yet know how good He is. We only know that His sweetness makes us long for more.

C. H. Spurgeon

There is wonderful freedom and joy in coming to recognize that the fun is in the becoming.

Gloria Gaither

God's plan for our guidance is for us to grow gradually in wisdom before we get to the crossroads.

Bill Hybels

A SUMMERTIME TIP

When it comes to your faith, God doesn't intend for you to stand still. He wants you to keep moving and growing throughout this summer and beyond.

THE RIGHT KIND OF FEAR

The fear of the Lord is the beginning of knowledge.
Proverbs 1:7 Holman CSB

Does every member of your family have a healthy, fearful respect for God's power? If so, you are wise. Genuine wisdom begins with a profound appreciation for God's limitless power.

God praises humility and punishes pride. That's why God's greatest servants will always be those humble men and women who care less for their own glory and more for God's glory. In God's kingdom, the only way to achieve greatness is to shun it. And the only way to be wise is to understand these facts: God is great; He is all-knowing; and He is all-powerful. We must respect Him, and we must humbly obey His commandments, or we must accept the consequences of our misplaced pride.

MORE THOUGHTS ABOUT
THE FEAR OF GOD

The remarkable thing about fearing God is that when you fear God, you fear nothing else, whereas if you do not fear God, you fear everything else.

Oswald Chambers

When true believers are awed by the greatness of God and by the privilege of becoming His children, then they become sincerely motivated, effective evangelists.

Bill Hybels

REMEMBER THIS

If you have a healthy fear of God, you're wise—if you don't, you're not.

STAYING FIT THIS SUMMER

Whatever you eat or drink or whatever you do,
you must do all for the glory of God.
1 Corinthians 10:31 NLT

The summer is a perfect time to shape up. So here's the big question: are you shaping up or spreading out? Do you eat sensibly and exercise regularly, or do you spend most of your time on the couch with a Twinkie in one hand and a clicker in the other? Are you choosing to treat your body like a temple or a trash heap? How you answer these questions will help determine how long you live and how well you live.

Physical fitness is a choice, a choice that requires discipline—it's as simple as that. So, do yourselves this favor: treat your bodies like one-of-a-kind gifts from God . . . because that's precisely what your bodies are.

MORE THOUGHTS ABOUT FITNESS

Jesus Christ is the One by whom, for whom, through whom everything was made. Therefore, He knows what's wrong in your life and how to fix it.

Anne Graham Lotz

A Christian should no more defile his body than a Jew would defile the temple.

Warren Wiersbe

SOMETHING TO THINK ABOUT

Simply put, it's up to you to assume the ultimate responsibility for your health. So if you're fighting the battle of the bulge (the bulging waistline, that is), don't waste your time blaming the fast food industry—or anybody else, for that matter. It's your body, and it's your responsibility to take care of it.

REAL WISDOM

Who is wise and understanding among you?
He should show his works by good conduct
with wisdom's gentleness.

James 3:13 Holman CSB

The ultimate source of wisdom is the Holy Word of God. If we call upon our Lord and seek to see the world through His eyes, He will give us guidance, wisdom, and perspective. When we make God's priorities our priorities, He will lead us according to His plan and according to His commandments. When we study God's Word, we are reminded that God's reality is the ultimate reality. But sometimes, when the demands of the day threaten to overwhelm us, we lose perspective, and we forfeit the blessings that God bestows upon those who accept His wisdom and His peace.

Do you seek to live according to God's plan? If so, you must study His Word. You must seek out worthy teachers and listen carefully to their advice. You must associate, day in and day out, with godly men and women. Then, as you accumulate wisdom, you must not keep it for yourself; you must, instead, share it with others.

But be forewarned: if you sincerely seek to share your hard-earned wisdom with the world, your actions must give credence to your words. The best way to share one's wisdom—perhaps the only way—is not by words, but by example.

MORE THOUGHTS ABOUT WISDOM

Wisdom takes us beyond the realm of mere right and wrong. Wisdom takes into account our personalities, our strengths, our weaknesses, and even our present state of mind.

Charles Stanley

All the knowledge you want is comprised in one book, the Bible.

John Wesley

Wise people listen to wise instruction, especially instruction from the Word of God.

Warren Wiersbe

If we neglect the Bible, we cannot expect to benefit from the wisdom and direction that result from knowing God's Word.

Vonette Bright

The wonderful thing about God's schoolroom is that we get to grade our own papers. You see, He doesn't test us so He can learn how well we're doing. He tests us so we can discover how well we're doing.

Charles Swindoll

A SUMMERTIME TIP

This season, like every season, God makes His wisdom available to you. Your job is to acknowledge, to understand, and (above all) to use that wisdom.

EMBRACING
GOD'S LOVE

The one who trusts in the Lord will have
faithful love surrounding him.

Psalm 32:10 Holman CSB

The words of 1 John 4:8 teach us that "He who does not love does not know God, for God is love" (NKJV). And because we can be assured that God is love, we can also be assured that God's heart is a loving heart.

God loves every member of your family. He loves you more than you can imagine; His affection is deeper than you can fathom. God made you in His own image and gave you salvation through the person of His Son Jesus Christ. And as a result, you and your loved ones have an important decision to make. You must decide what to do about God's love: you can return it . . . or not.

When you accept the love that flows from the heart of God, you are transformed. When you embrace God's love, you feel differently about yourselves, your family, your neighbors, your community, your church, and your world. When you open your heart to God's love, you will feel compelled to share God's message—and His compassion—with others.

Corrie ten Boom observed, "We must mirror God's love in the midst of a world full of hatred. We are the mirrors of God's love, so we may show Jesus by our lives." And her words most certainly apply to every Christian family, including yours.

God's heart is overflowing with love for you and yours. Accept that love. Return that love. Respect that love. And share that love. Today.

MORE THOUGHTS ABOUT GOD'S LOVE

If you have an obedience problem, you have a love problem. Focus your attention on God's love.

Henry Blackaby

Even when we cannot see the why and wherefore of God's dealings, we know that there is love in and behind them, so we can rejoice always.

J. I. Packer

The life of faith is a daily exploration of the constant and countless ways in which God's grace and love are experienced.

Eugene Peterson

Jesus loves us with fidelity, purity, constancy, and passion, no matter how imperfect we are.

Stormie Omartian

There is no pit so deep that God's love is not deeper still.

Corrie ten Boom

REMEMBER THIS

When all else fails, God's love does not. You can always depend upon God's love . . . and He is always your ultimate protection.

FORGIVENESS NOW

For if you forgive people their wrongdoing,
your heavenly Father will forgive you as well.
But if you don't forgive people,
your Father will not forgive your wrongdoing.
Matthew 6:14-15 Holman CSB

This season, like every season, is the right time to forgive. So if you want to have a great summer, make forgiveness a high priority.

How often must we forgive our family members and friends? More times than we can count. Our friends and family members are imperfect; so are we. So all of us must, on occasion, forgive those who have injured us; to do otherwise is to disobey God.

If there exists even one person, alive or dead, whom you have not forgiven (and that includes yourself), follow God's commandment and His will for your life: forgive. Hatred, bitterness, and regret are not part of God's plan for your life . . . forgiveness is.

MORE THOUGHTS ABOUT FORGIVENESS

Two works of mercy set a man free: forgive and you will be forgiven, and give and you will receive.

St. Augustine

I believe that forgiveness can become a continuing cycle: because God forgives us, we're to forgive others; because we forgive others, God forgives us. Scripture presents both parts of the cycle.

Shirley Dobson

SOMETHING TO THINK ABOUT

Forgiveness is its own reward. Bitterness is its own punishment. Guard your words and your thoughts accordingly.

23

EXPERIENCING GOD'S ABUNDANCE THIS SUMMER

I have come that they may have life,
and that they may have it more abundantly.
John 10:10 NKJV

Does your family seek God's abundance? Of course you do. And it's worth remembering that God's rewards are most certainly available to you and yours. The 10th chapter of John tells us that Christ came to earth so that our lives might be filled with abundance. But what, exactly, did Jesus mean when He promised "life . . . more abundantly"? Was He referring to material possessions or financial wealth? Hardly. Jesus offers a different kind of abundance: a spiritual richness that extends beyond the temporal boundaries of this world. This everlasting abundance is available to all who seek it and claim it. May your family claim those riches, and may you share Christ's blessings with all who cross your path.

MORE THOUGHTS ABOUT ABUNDANCE

If we were given all we wanted here, our hearts would settle for this world rather than the next.

Elisabeth Elliot

Jesus intended for us to be overwhelmed by the blessings of regular days. He said it was the reason He had come: "I am come that they might have life, and that they might have it more abundantly."

Gloria Gaither

REMEMBER THIS

Abundance and obedience go hand-in-hand. Obey God first and expect to receive His abundance second, not vice versa.

SUMMERTIME: A PERFECT TIME FOR FAMILY

*We can't afford to waste a minute, must not squander
these precious daylight hours in frivolity and indulgence,
in sleeping around and dissipation, in bickering and
grabbing everything in sight. Get out of bed and get
dressed! Don't loiter and linger, waiting until
the very last minute. Dress yourselves in Christ,
and be up and about!*
Romans 13:13-14 MSG

I t takes time to build strong family ties . . . lots of
time. Yet we live in a world where time seems to
be an ever-shrinking commodity as we rush from
place to place with seldom a moment to spare.

Has the busy pace of life robbed you of
sufficient time with your loved ones? If so, it's time
to fine-tune your priorities. And God can help.

When you make God a full partner in every
aspect of your life, He will lead you along the proper
path: His path. When you allow God to reign over

your life, He will enrich your relationships and your life. So, as you plan for the day ahead, make God's priorities your priorities. When you do, every other priority will have a tendency to fall neatly into place.

MORE THOUGHTS ABOUT SPENDING TIME WITH LOVED ONES

I don't buy the cliché that quality time is the most important thing. If you don't have enough quantity, you won't get quality.

Leighton Ford

The more time you give to something, the more you reveal its importance and value to you.

Rick Warren

Overcommitment and time pressures are the greatest destroyers of marriages and families. It takes time to develop any friendship, whether with a loved one or with God himself.

James Dobson

What really builds togetherness is time spent together—lots of time.

Dennis Swanberg

As we surrender the use of our time to the lordship of Christ, He will lead us to use it in the most productive way imaginable.

Charles Stanley

A SUMMERTIME TIP

Summertime, like every other season of the year, is the right time to spend time with family. Chuck Swindoll has simple advice: "Never give your family the leftovers and crumbs of your time." And he's right.

25

WHO'S FIRST?

Do not have other gods besides Me.
Exodus 20:3 Holman CSB

As you think about the nature of your relationship with God, remember this: you will always have some type of relationship with Him—it is inevitable that your life must be lived in relationship to God. The question is not if you will have a relationship with Him; the burning question is whether that relationship will be one that seeks to honor Him . . . or not.

Does your family put God first? And, are you willing to welcome God's Son into your heart? Unless you can honestly answer these questions with a resounding yes, then your relationship with God isn't what it could be or should be. Thankfully, God is always available, He's always ready to forgive, and He's waiting to hear from you now. The rest, of course, is up to you.

MORE THOUGHTS ABOUT
PUTTING GOD FIRST

Our ultimate aim in life is not to be healthy, wealthy, prosperous, or problem free. Our ultimate aim in life is to bring glory to God.

Anne Graham Lotz

When all else is gone, God is still left. Nothing changes Him.

Hannah Whitall Smith

REMEMBER THIS

God deserves first place in your family . . . and you deserve the experience of putting Him there.

ANSWERING THE CALL
THIS SUMMER

I, therefore, the prisoner in the Lord, urge you to walk worthy of the calling you have received.

Ephesians 4:1 Holman CSB

It is vitally important that your family heed God's call. In John 15:16, Jesus says, "You did not choose me, but I chose you and appointed you to go and bear fruit—fruit that will last" (NIV). In other words, your clan has been called by Christ, and now, it is up to you to decide precisely how you will answer.

As a family, are you sincerely searching for that special calling? If so, you are both fortunate and wise. If not, keep searching and keep praying until you discover it. And remember this: God has important work for your family—specific work, important work, critical work that no other family on earth can accomplish but yours.

MORE THOUGHTS ABOUT GOD'S CALLING

The world does not consider labor a blessing, therefore it flees and hates it, but the pious who fear the Lord labor with a ready and cheerful heart, for they know God's command, and they acknowledge His calling.

Martin Luther

If God has called you, do not spend time looking over your shoulder to see who is following you.

Corrie ten Boom

REMEMBER THIS

God has a plan for your family, a divine calling that you can either answer or ignore. How you choose to respond to God's calling will determine the direction you take and the contributions you make.

A Summer of Prayer

Don't worry about anything, but in everything,
through prayer and petition with thanksgiving,
let your requests be made known to God.
Philippians 4:6 Holman CSB

If you want to experience a terrific summer, you'll need to make this season a time of prayer.

Does your family pray together often or just at church? Are you a little band of prayer warriors, or have you retreated from God's battlefield? Do you and yours pray only at mealtimes, or do you pray much more often than that? The answer to these questions will determine, to a surprising extent, the level of your family's spiritual health.

Jesus made it clear to His disciples: they should pray always. And so should you. Genuine, heartfelt prayer changes things and it changes you. When you lift your heart to the Father, you open yourself to a never-ending source of divine wisdom and infinite love.

Your family's prayers are powerful. So, as you go about your daily activities, remember God's instructions: "Rejoice always! Pray constantly. Give thanks in everything, for this is God's will for you in Christ Jesus" (1 Thessalonians 5:16-18 Holman CSB). Start praying in the morning and keep praying until you fall off to sleep at night. And rest assured: God is always listening, and He always wants to hear from you and your family.

MORE THOUGHTS ABOUT PRAYER

When there is a matter that requires definite prayer, pray until you believe God and until you can thank Him for His answer.

Hannah Whitall Smith

I live in the spirit of prayer; I pray as I walk, when I lie down, and when I rise. And, the answers are always coming.

George Mueller

God delights in the prayers of His children—prayers that express our love for Him, prayers that share our deepest burdens with Him.

Billy Graham

Pour out your heart to God and tell Him how you feel. Be real, be honest, and when you get it all out, you'll start to feel the gradual covering of God's comforting presence.

Bill Hybels

As we join together in prayer, we draw on God's enabling might in a way that multiplies our own efforts many times over.

Shirley Dobson

SOMETHING TO THINK ABOUT

Today, think about the role that prayer does play, and the role that it should play, in the life of your family.

GOD CAN HANDLE IT

For I, the Lord your God, hold your right hand
and say to you: Do not fear, I will help you.
Isaiah 41:13 Holman CSB

It's a promise that is made over and over again in the Bible: Whatever "it" is, God can handle it.

Life isn't always easy. Far from it! Sometimes, life can be very, very tough. But even then, even during our darkest moments, we're protected by a loving Heavenly Father. When we're worried, God can reassure us; when we're sad, God can comfort us. When our hearts are broken, God is not just near, He is here. So we must lift our thoughts and prayers to Him. When we do, He will answer our prayers. Why? Because He is our shepherd, and He has promised to protect us now and forever.

MORE THOUGHTS ABOUT GOD'S PROTECTION

God uses our most stumbling, faltering faith-steps as the open door to His doing for us "more than we ask or think."

Catherine Marshall

God is always sufficient in perfect proportion to our need.

Beth Moore

We are never out of reach of Satan's devices, so we must never be without the whole armor of God.

Warren Wiersbe

REMEMBER THIS

You are protected by God . . . now and always. The only security that lasts is the security that flows from the loving heart of God.

29

HE'S HERE

Draw near to God, and He will draw near to you.

James 4:8 Holman CSB

Since God is everywhere, we are free to sense His presence whenever we take the time to quiet our souls and turn our prayers to Him. But sometimes, amid the incessant demands of life, we turn our thoughts far from God; when we do, we suffer.

Do you schedule a regular meeting each day with your Creator? You should. During these moments of stillness, you will gain direction, perspective, and peace—God's peace.

The comforting words of Psalm 46:10 remind us to "Be still, and know that I am God." When we do so, we sense the loving presence of our Heavenly Father, and we are comforted by the certain knowledge that God is not far away . . . and He isn't even nearby. He is, quite literally, here. And it's up to each of us to sense His presence.

MORE THOUGHTS ABOUT GOD'S PRESENCE

Our souls were made to live in an upper atmosphere, and we stifle and choke if we live on any lower level. Our eyes were made to look off from these heavenly heights, and our vision is distorted by any lower gazing.

Hannah Whitall Smith

We are never more fulfilled than when our longing for God is met by His presence in our lives.

Billy Graham

God expresses His love toward us by His uninterrupted presence in our lives.

Charles Stanley

Whatever hallway you're in—no matter how long, how dark, or how scary—God is right there with you.

Bill Hybels

If your heart has grown cold, it is because you have moved away from the fire of His presence.

Beth Moore

If you want to hear God's voice clearly and you are uncertain, then remain in His presence until He changes that uncertainty. Often, much can happen during this waiting for the Lord. Sometimes, He changes pride into humility, doubt into faith and peace.

Corrie ten Boom

REMEMBER THIS

God isn't far away—He's right here, right now. And He's willing to talk to you right here, right now.

30

DOING THE RIGHT THINGS ALL SUMMER LONG

So we must not get tired of doing good, for we will reap at the proper time if we don't give up.

Galatians 6:9 Holman CSB

D o you want to have a great summer? Then make sure that your actions are pleasing to God.

Oswald Chambers, the author of the Christian classic *My Utmost for His Highest*, advised, "Never support an experience which does not have God as its source, and faith in God as its result." These words serve as a powerful reminder that, as Christians, we are called to walk with God and obey His commandments. But, we live in a world that presents countless temptations for adults and children alike.

We Christians, when confronted with sin, have clear instructions: walk—or better yet run—in the opposite direction. When we do, we reap the blessings that God has promised to all those who live according to His will and His word.

MORE THOUGHTS ABOUT DOING WHAT'S RIGHT

Although God causes all things to work together for good for His children, He still holds us accountable for our behavior.

Kay Arthur

Either God's Word keeps you from sin, or sin keeps you from God's Word.

Corrie ten Boom

There may be no trumpet sound or loud applause when we make a right decision, just a calm sense of resolution and peace.

Gloria Gaither

Live in such a way that any day would make a suitable capstone for life. Live so that you need not change your mode of living, even if your sudden departure were immediately predicted to you.

C. H. Spurgeon

More depends on my walk than my talk.

D. L. Moody

Our response to God determines His response to us.

Henry Blackaby

A SUMMERTIME TIP

Ask yourself if your behavior has been radically changed by your unfolding relationship with God. If the answer to this question is unclear to you—or if the honest answer is a resounding no—think of a single step you can take this summer, a positive change in your life, that will bring you closer to your Creator.

TRUSTING GOD'S TIMETABLE THIS SUMMER

He has made everything appropriate in its time. He has also put eternity in their hearts, but man cannot discover the work God has done from beginning to end.

Ecclesiastes 3:11 Holman CSB

We should learn to trust God's timing, but we are sorely tempted to do otherwise. Why? Because we human beings are usually anxious for things to happen sooner rather than later. But, God knows better.

God has created a world that unfolds according to His own timetable, not ours . . . thank goodness! We mortals might make a terrible mess of things. God does not. God's plan does not always happen in the way that we would like or at the time of our own choosing. Our task is to wait patiently and never lose hope.

In the words of Elisabeth Elliot, "We must learn to move according to the timetable of the Timeless

One, and to be at peace." That's advice worth following this summer and in every season of life.

MORE THOUGHTS ABOUT GOD'S TIMING

He has the right to interrupt your life. He is Lord. When you accepted Him as Lord, you gave Him the right to help Himself to your life anytime He wants.

Henry Blackaby

When there is perplexity there is always guidance—not always at the moment we ask, but in good time, which is God's time. There is no need to fret and stew.

Elisabeth Elliot

Your times are in His hands. He's in charge of the timetable, so wait patiently.

Kay Arthur

Waiting on God brings us to the journey's end quicker than our feet.

Mrs. Charles E. Cowman

God never hurries. There are no deadlines against which He must work. To know this is to quiet our spirits and relax our nerves.

A. W. Tozer

You're in a hurry. God is not. Trust God.

Marie T. Freeman

SOMETHING TO THINK ABOUT

God has very big plans in store for your family, so trust Him and wait patiently for those plans to unfold. And remember: God's timing is best.

ESTABLISHING HEALTHY HABITS THIS SUMMER

Do not be deceived:
"Evil company corrupts good habits."
1 Corinthians 15:33 NKJV

The summertime is a great time to establish new, healthier habits. So why not start today?

As the old saying goes: "First, you make your habits, and then your habits make you." Some habits will inevitably bring you closer to God; other habits will lead you away from the path He has chosen for you. If you sincerely desire to improve your spiritual health, you must honestly examine the habits that make up the fabric of your day. And you must abandon those habits that are displeasing to God.

If you trust God, and if you keep asking for His help, He can transform your life. If you sincerely ask Him to help you, the same God who created the universe will help you defeat the harmful habits that have heretofore defeated you. So, if at first you don't succeed, keep praying. God is listening, and He's ready to help you become a better person if you ask Him . . . so ask today.

MORE THOUGHTS ABOUT HABITS

Since behaviors become habits, make them work with you and not against you.

E. Stanley Jones

REMEMBER THIS

Target your most unhealthy habit first, and attack it with vigor. When it comes to defeating harmful habitual behaviors, you'll need focus, determination, prayer, more focus, more determination, and more prayer.

FINDING HAPPINESS
THIS SUMMER

How happy is everyone who fears the Lord,
who walks in His ways!
Psalm 128:1 Holman CSB

Happiness depends less upon our circumstances than upon our thoughts. When we turn our thoughts to God, to His gifts, and to His glorious creation, we experience the joy that God intends for His children. But, when we focus on the negative aspects of life, we inadvertently bring needless pain to our friends, to our families, and to ourselves.

Do you sincerely want to be a happy? Then set your mind and your heart upon God's love and His grace. Seek a genuine, intimate, life-altering relationship with your Creator by studying His Word and trusting His promises. And while you're at it, count your blessings instead of your hardships. Then, after you've done these things, claim the joy, the peace, and the spiritual abundance that the Shepherd offers His sheep.

MORE THOUGHTS ABOUT HAPPINESS

Christ is the secret, the source, the substance, the center, and the circumference of all true and lasting gladness.

Mrs. Charles E. Cowman

I became aware of one very important concept I had missed before: my attitude—not my circumstances—was what was making me unhappy.

Vonette Bright

SOMETHING TO THINK ABOUT

If you want to find lasting happiness, don't chase it. Instead, do your duty, obey your God, and wait for happiness to find you.

FINDING HOPE THIS SUMMER

*Now may the God of hope fill you with all joy
and peace in believing, so that you may overflow with
hope by the power of the Holy Spirit.*
Romans 15:13 Holman CSB

Despite God's promises, despite Christ's love, and despite our countless blessings, we frail human beings can still lose hope from time to time. When we do, we need the encouragement of Christian friends, the life-changing power of prayer, and the healing truth of God's Holy Word.

If you find yourself falling into the spiritual traps of worry and discouragement, seek the healing touch of Jesus and the encouraging words of fellow Christians. And remember the words of our Savior: "These things I have spoken unto you, that in me ye might have peace. In the world ye shall have tribulation: but be of good cheer; I have overcome the world" (John 16:33 KJV). This world can be a place of trials and tribulations, but as believers, we are secure. God has promised us peace, joy, and eternal life. And, of course, God keeps His promises today, tomorrow, and forever.

MORE THOUGHTS ABOUT HOPE

Faith looks back and draws courage; hope looks ahead and keeps desire alive.

John Eldredge

Never yield to gloomy anticipation. Place your hope and confidence in God. He has no record of failure.

Mrs. Charles E. Cowman

I wish I could make it all new again; I can't. But God can. "He restores my soul," wrote the shepherd. God doesn't reform; He restores. He doesn't camouflage the old; He restores the new. The Master Builder will pull out the original plan and restore it. He will restore the vigor, He will restore the energy. He will restore the hope. He will restore the soul.

Max Lucado

Oh, remember this: There is never a time when we may not hope in God. Whatever our necessities, however great our difficulties, and though to all appearance help is impossible, yet our business is to hope in God, and it will be found that it is not in vain.

George Mueller

Hope must be in the future tense. Faith, to be faith, must always be in the present tense.

Catherine Marshall

REMEMBER THIS

Since God has promised to guide and protect you—now and forever—you should never lose hope.

35

THE WISDOM TO BE HUMBLE

Therefore, God's chosen ones, holy and loved,
put on heartfelt compassion, kindness, humility,
gentleness, and patience.

Colossians 3:12 Holman CSB

Humility is not, in most cases, a naturally occurring human trait. Most of us, it seems, are more than willing to overestimate our own accomplishments. We are tempted to say, "Look how wonderful I am!" . . . hoping all the while that the world will agree with our own self-appraisals. But those of us who fall prey to the sin of pride should beware—God is definitely not impressed by our prideful proclamations.

God honors humility . . . and He rewards those who humbly serve Him. So if you've acquired the wisdom to be humble, then you are to be congratulated. But if you've not yet overcome the tendency to overestimate your own accomplishments, then God still has some important (and perhaps painful) lessons to teach you—lessons about humility that you still need to learn.

MORE THOUGHTS ABOUT HUMILITY

It was pride that changed angels into devils; it is humility that makes men as angels.

St. Augustine

Humility is not thinking less of yourself; it is thinking of yourself less.

Rick Warren

SOMETHING TO THINK ABOUT

You must remain humble or face the consequences. Pride does go before the fall, but humility often prevents the fall.

36

HIS JOY AND YOURS

A joyful heart is good medicine,
but a broken spirit dries up the bones.
Proverbs 17:22 Holman CSB

Christ made it clear: He intends that His joy sould become our joy. Yet sometimes, amid the inevitable hustle and bustle of life here on earth, we can forfeit—albeit temporarily—the joy of Christ as we wrestle with the challenges of daily living.

Jonathan Edwards, the 18th-century American clergyman, observed, "Christ is not only a remedy for your weariness and trouble, but He will give you an abundance of the contrary: joy and delight. They who come to Christ do not only come to a resting-place after they have been wandering in a wilderness, but they come to a banqueting-house where they may rest, and where they may feast. They may cease from their former troubles and toils, and they may enter upon a course of delights and spiritual joys."

If, today, your heart is heavy, open the door of your soul to Christ. He will give you peace and joy. And, if you already have the joy of Christ in your heart, share it freely, just as Christ freely shared His joy with you.

MORE THOUGHTS ABOUT JOY

What is your focus today? Joy comes when it is Jesus first, others second . . . then you.

Kay Arthur

The Christian lifestyle is not one of legalistic do's and don'ts, but one that is positive, attractive, and joyful.

Vonette Bright

Joy is the direct result of having God's perspective on our daily lives and the effect of loving our Lord enough to obey His commands and trust His promises.

Bill Bright

Joy is the heart's harmonious response to the Lord's song of love.

A. W. Tozer

Our sense of joy, satisfaction, and fulfillment in life increases, no matter what the circumstances, if we are in the center of God's will.

Billy Graham

Lord, I thank you for the promise of heaven and the unexpected moments when you touch my heartstrings with that longing for my eternal home.

Joni Eareckson Tada

REMEMBER THIS

Joy does not depend upon your circumstances; it depends upon your thoughts and upon your relationship with God.

37

LOOKING FOR MIRACLES THIS SUMMER

You are the God who works wonders;
You revealed Your strength among the peoples.
Psalm 77:14 Holman CSB

D o you believe that God is at work in the world? And do you also believe that nothing is impossible for Him? If so, then you also believe that God is perfectly capable of doing things that you, as a mere human being with limited vision and limited understanding, would deem to be utterly impossible. And that's precisely what God does.

Since the moment that He created our universe out of nothingness, God has made a habit of doing miraculous things. And He still works miracles today. Expect Him to work miracles in your own lives, and then be watchful. With God, absolutely nothing is impossible, including an amazing assortment of miracles that He stands ready, willing, and able to perform for you and yours.

MORE THOUGHTS ABOUT MIRACLES

Miracles are not contrary to nature but only contrary to what we know about nature.

St. Augustine

Only God can move mountains, but faith and prayer can move God.

E. M. Bounds

Too many Christians live below the miracle level.

Vance Havner

A SUMMERTIME TIP

God has infinite power. If you're watchful, you'll observe many miracles. So make sure this summer to keep your eyes, your hearts, and your minds open.

WORSHIP HIM

Worship the Lord your God and . . . serve Him only.
Matthew 4:10 Holman CSB

Why does your family attend church? Is it because of your sincere desire to worship and to praise God? Hopefully so. Yet far too many Christians attend worship services because they believe they are "supposed to go to church" or because they feel "pressured" to attend. Still others go to church for "social" reasons. But make no mistake: the best reason to attend church is out of a sincere desire to please God, to praise God, to experience God, and to discern God's will for your life.

Some people may tell you that they don't engage in worship. Don't believe them. All of mankind is engaged in worship. The question is not whether we worship, but what we worship. Wise folks choose to worship God. When they do, they are blessed with a plentiful harvest of joy, peace, and abundance. Other people choose to distance themselves from God by foolishly worshiping things that are intended to bring personal gratification but not spiritual gratification. Such choices often have tragic consequences.

How can we ensure that we cast our lot with God? We do so, in part, by the practice of regular, purposeful worship in the company of fellow believers. And we must worship our Heavenly Father not just with our words, but also with deeds. We must honor Him, praise Him, and obey Him. As we seek to find purpose and meaning for our lives, we must first seek His purpose and His will. For believers, God comes first. Always first.

MORE THOUGHTS ABOUT WORSHIP

God actually delights in and pursues our worship (Proverbs 15:8 & John 4:23).

Shirley Dobson

To worship Him in truth means to worship Him honestly, without hypocrisy, standing open and transparent before Him.

Anne Graham Lotz

Inside the human heart is an undeniable, spiritual instinct to commune with its Creator.

Jim Cymbala

Worship is a daunting task. Each worships differently. But each should worship.

Max Lucado

God asks that we worship Him with our concentrated minds as well as with our wills and emotions. A divided and scattered mind is not effective.

Catherine Marshall

A SUMMERTIME TIP

Make this summer a time of sincere worship. When you worship God with a sincere heart, He will guide your steps and bless your life.

OBEDIENCE NOW

For it is God who is working among you both the willing and the working for His good purpose.
Philippians 2:13 Holman CSB

God has given us a guidebook for abundant life; that book is the Holy Bible. It contains thorough instructions which, if followed, lead to fulfillment, righteousness, and salvation. But, if we choose to ignore God's commandments, the results are as predictable as they are tragic.

How can we demonstrate our love for God? By placing Christ squarely at the center of our lives. Jesus said that if we are to love Him, we must obey His commandments (John 14:15). Thus, our obedience to the Master is an expression of our love for Him.

In Ephesians 2:10 we read, "For we are His workmanship, created in Christ Jesus for good works" (NKJV). These words are instructive: We are not saved by good works, but for good works. Good works are not the root, but rather the fruit of our salvation.

When we seek righteousness in our own lives—and when we seek the companionship of those who do likewise—we reap the spiritual rewards that God intends for our lives. When we behave ourselves as godly people, we honor God. When we live righteously and according to God's commandments, He blesses us in ways that we cannot fully understand.

As families, we should take every step of our journey with God. We should continue to read His Word, and we should continue to follow His commandments. We should support only those activities that further God's kingdom and our own spiritual growth. And we should be worthy examples to our friends and neighbors. When we do, we'll reap the blessings that God has promised to all those who live according to His will and His Word.

MORE THOUGHTS ABOUT OBEDIENCE

God is God. Because He is God, He is worthy of my trust and obedience. I will find rest nowhere but in His holy will, a will that is unspeakably beyond my largest notions of what He is up to.

Elisabeth Elliot

The pathway of obedience can sometimes be difficult, but it always leads to a strengthening of our inner woman.

Vonette Bright

Believe and do what God says. The life-changing consequences will be limitless, and the results will be confidence and peace of mind.

Franklin Graham

Obedience is the outward expression of your love of God.

Henry Blackaby

REMEMBER THIS

God has rules. When we follow them, we are blessed; when we ignore them, we are harmed.

40

THE POWER OF PERSEVERANCE

For you need endurance, so that after you have done
God's will, you may receive what was promised.
Hebrews 10:36 Holman CSB

L ife's occasional disappointments are inevitable.
Such setbacks are simply the price that we must
pay for our willingness to take risks as we follow
our dreams. But even when we encounter setbacks,
we must never lose faith.

In a world filled with roadblocks and stumbling
blocks, we need strength, courage, and perseverance.
The reassuring words of Hebrews 10:36 serve as a
comforting reminder that perseverance indeed
pays.

Are you willing to trust God's Word? And are
you willing to keep "fighting the good fight," even
when you've experienced unexpected difficulties? If
so, you may soon be surprised at the creative ways
that God finds to help determined people like you
. . . people who possess the wisdom and the courage
to persevere.

MORE THOUGHTS ABOUT PERSEVERANCE

Jesus taught that perseverance is the essential element in prayer.

E. M. Bounds

Perseverance is more than endurance. It is endurance combined with absolute assurance and certainty that what we are looking for is going to happen.

Oswald Chambers

Battles are won in the trenches, in the grit and grime of courageous determination; they are won day by day in the arena of life.

Charles Swindoll

Are you a Christian? If you are, how can you be hopeless? Are you so depressed by the greatness of your problems that you have given up all hope? Instead of giving up, would you patiently endure? Would you focus on Christ until you are so preoccupied with Him alone that you fall prostrate before Him?

Anne Graham Lotz

If things are tough, remember that every flower that ever bloomed had to go through a whole lot of dirt to get there.

Barbara Johnson

We are all on our way somewhere. We'll get there if we just keep going.

Barbara Johnson

REMEMBER THIS

Life is, at times, difficult. When you are tested, call upon God. He can give you the strength to persevere, and that's exactly what you should ask Him to do.

THE WISDOM
TO BE GRATEFUL

Let the message about the Messiah dwell richly among
you, teaching and admonishing one another in
all wisdom, and singing psalms, hymns, and spiritual
songs, with gratitude in your hearts to God.

Colossians 3:16 Holman CSB

For most of us, life is busy and complicated. We have countless responsibilities, some of which begin before sunrise and many of which end long after sunset. Amid the rush and crush of the daily grind, it is easy to lose sight of God and His blessings. But, when we forget to slow down and say "Thank You" to our Maker, we rob ourselves of His presence, His peace, and His joy.

Our task—as the leaders of our families and as believing Christians—is to praise God many times each day. Then, with gratitude in our hearts, we can face our daily duties with the perspective and power that only He can provide.

MORE THOUGHTS ABOUT GRATITUDE

Gratitude changes the pangs of memory into a tranquil joy.

Dietrich Bonhoeffer

If you won't fill your heart with gratitude, the devil will fill it with something else.

Marie T. Freeman

It is only with gratitude that life becomes rich.

Dietrich Bonhoeffer

A SUMMERTIME TIP

Developing an attitude of gratitude is key to a joyful summer and satisfying life. So ask yourself this question: "Am I grateful enough?"

KINDNESS IS A CHOICE

A kind man benefits himself,
but a cruel man brings disaster on himself.

Proverbs 11:17 Holman CSB

Where does kindness start? It starts in our hearts and our homes . . . and then it works its way out from there. Jesus taught us that a pure heart is a wonderful blessing. It's up to each of us to fill our hearts with love for God, love for Jesus, and love for all people. When we do, we are blessed.

Do you want to experience a terrific summer? Then invite the Father's love into your heart and share it with family and friends. After all, your Creator has blessed you in countless ways, and He has instructed you to share your blessings with the world. So today, look for opportunities to spread kindness wherever you go. God deserves no less, and neither, for that matter, do your loved ones.

MORE THOUGHTS ABOUT KINDNESS

Be so preoccupied with good will that you haven't room for ill will.

E. Stanley Jones

When you extend hospitality to others, you're not trying to impress people, you're trying to reflect God to them.

Max Lucado

If we have the true love of God in our hearts, we will show it in our lives. We will not have to go up and down the earth proclaiming it. We will show it in everything we say or do.

D. L. Moody

When we do little acts of kindness that make life more bearable for someone else, we are walking in love as the Bible commands us.

Barbara Johnson

A little kindly advice is better than a great deal of scolding.

Fanny Crosby

Do all the good you can. By all the means you can.
In all the ways you can. In all the places you can.
At all the times you can. To all the people you can.
As long as ever you can.

John Wesley

A SUMMERTIME TIP

Want to have more fun this summer?
Then try being a little kinder this
summer.

HE RENEWS YOUR STRENGTH

I will give you a new heart and
put a new spirit within you.
Ezekiel 36:26 Holman CSB

This summer, like every season of life, is literally brimming with possibilities. Whether we realize it or not, God is always working in us and through us; our job is to let Him do His work without undue interference. Yet we are imperfect beings who, because of our limited vision, often resist God's will. We want life to unfold according to our own desires, not God's. But, our Heavenly Father may have other plans.

For busy people living in a fast-paced 21st-century world, life may seem like a merry-go-round that never stops turning. If that description seems to fit your life, then you may find yourself running short of patience or strength, or both. If you're feeling tired or discouraged, there is a source from which you can draw the power needed to renew your spirit and your strength. That source is God.

MORE THOUGHTS ABOUT RENEWAL

Walking with God leads to receiving His intimate counsel, and counseling leads to deep restoration.

John Eldredge

Jesus is calling the weary to rest, / Calling today, calling today, / Bring Him your burden and you shall be blest; / He will not turn you away.

Fanny Crosby

God specializes in things fresh and firsthand. His plans for you this year may outshine those of the past. He's prepared to fill your days with reasons to give Him praise.

Joni Eareckson Tada

If you're willing to repair your life, God is willing to help. If you're not willing to repair your life, God is willing to wait.

Marie T. Freeman

He is the God of wholeness and restoration.

Stormie Omartian

117

But while relaxation is one thing, refreshment is another. We need to drink frequently and at length from God's fresh springs, to spend time in the Scripture, time in fellowship with Him, time worshiping Him.

Ruth Bell Graham

REMEMBER THIS

God can make all things new, including you. When you are weak or worried, God can renew your spirit. Your task is to let Him.

LISTEN CAREFULLY

The one who is from God listens to God's words.
This is why you don't listen,
because you are not from God.
John 8:47 Holman CSB

Sometimes God speaks loudly and clearly. More often, He speaks in a quiet voice—and if you are wise, you will be listening carefully when He does. To do so, you must carve out quiet moments each day to study His Word and sense His direction.

Can you quiet yourself long enough to listen to your conscience? Are you attuned to the subtle guidance of your intuition? Are you willing to pray sincerely and then to wait quietly for God's response? Hopefully so. Usually God refrains from sending His messages on stone tablets or city billboards. More often, He communicates in subtler ways. If you sincerely desire to hear His voice, you must listen carefully, and you must do so in the silent corners of your quiet, willing heart.

MORE THOUGHTS ABOUT
LISTENING TO GOD

When we come to Jesus stripped of pretensions, with a needy spirit, ready to listen, He meets us at the point of need.

Catherine Marshall

In the soul-searching of our lives, we are to stay quiet so we can hear Him say all that He wants to say to us in our hearts.

Charles Swindoll

A SUMMERTIME TIP

Is the noise of summer making it hard for you to hear God? If so, slow yourself down, tune out the distractions, and listen carefully. God has important things to say; your task is to be still and listen.

LOVE ACCORDING
TO GOD

Now these three remain: faith, hope, and love.
But the greatest of these is love.

1 Corinthians 13:13 Holman CSB

Love, like everything else in this wonderful world, begins and ends with God, but the middle part belongs to us. During the brief time that we have here on earth, God has given each of us the opportunity to become a loving person—or not. God has given each of us the opportunity to be kind, to be courteous, to be cooperative, and to be forgiving—or not. God has given each of us the chance to obey the Golden Rule, or to make up our own rules as we go. If we obey God's rules, we're safe, but if we do otherwise, we're headed for trouble and fast.

Here in the real world, the choices that we make have consequences. The decisions that we make and the results of those decisions determine the quality of our relationships. It's as simple as that.

MORE THOUGHTS ABOUT LOVE

Those who abandon ship the first time it enters a storm miss the calm beyond. And the rougher the storms weathered together, the deeper and stronger real love grows.

Ruth Bell Graham

It is when we come to the Lord in our nothingness, our powerlessness and our helplessness that He then enables us to love in a way which, without Him, would be absolutely impossible.

Elisabeth Elliot

Love is extravagant in the price it is willing to pay, the time it is willing to give, the hardships it is willing to endure, and the strength it is willing to spend. Love never thinks in terms of "how little," but always in terms of "how much." Love gives, love knows, and love lasts.

Joni Eareckson Tada

Love is an attribute of God. To love others is evidence of a genuine faith.

Kay Arthur

If Jesus is the preeminent One in our lives, then we will love each other, submit to each other, and treat one another fairly in the Lord.

Warren Wiersbe

Love simply cannot spring up without that self-surrender to each other. If either withholds the self, love cannot exist.

E. Stanley Jones

A SUMMERTIME TIP

This summer, make certain that love is expressed and demonstrated many times each day at your house. Little acts of kindness can make a big difference.

SHARING HIS PEACE

*And the peace of God, which surpasses every thought,
will guard your hearts and your minds in Christ
Jesus. Finally brothers, whatever is true, whatever is
honorable, whatever is just, whatever is pure, whatever
is lovely, whatever is commendable—if there is any
moral excellence and if there is any praise—
dwell on these things.*

Philippians 4:7-8 Holman CSB

On many occasions, our outer struggles are simply manifestations of the inner conflicts that we feel when we stray from God's path. What's needed is a refresher course in God's promise of peace. The beautiful words of John 14:27 remind us that Jesus offers peace, not as the world gives, but as He alone gives: "Peace I leave with you. My peace I give to you. I do not give to you as the world gives. Your heart must not be troubled or fearful" (Holman CSB).

As believers, our challenge is straightforward: we should welcome Christ's peace into our hearts and then, as best we can, share His peace with our neighbors.

This summer, invite Christ to preside over every aspect of your life. It's the best way to live and the surest path to peace . . . now and forever.

MORE THOUGHTS ABOUT PEACE

To know God as He really is—in His essential nature and character—is to arrive at a citadel of peace that circumstances may storm, but can never capture.

Catherine Marshall

Let's please God by actively seeking, through prayer, "peaceful and quiet lives" for ourselves, our spouses, our children and grandchildren, our friends, and our nation (1 Timothy 2:1-3 NIV).

Shirley Dobson

God's peace is like a river, not a pond. In other words, a sense of health and well-being, both of which are expressions of the Hebrew shalom, can permeate our homes even when we're in white-water rapids.

Beth Moore

A great many people are trying to make peace, but that has already been done. God has not left it for us to do; all we have to do is to enter into it.

D. L. Moody

In the center of a hurricane there is absolute quiet and peace. There is no safer place than in the center of the will of God.

Corrie ten Boom

The fruit of our placing all things in God's hands is the presence of His abiding peace in our hearts.

Hannah Whitall Smith

REMEMBER THIS

God's peace surpasses human understanding. When you accept His peace, it will revolutionize your life.

SEEKING
GOD'S GUIDANCE
THIS SUMMER

I will instruct you and show you the way to go;
with My eye on you, I will give counsel.

Psalm 32:8 Holman CSB

The Bible promises that God will guide your family if you let Him. Your job, of course, is to let Him. But sometimes, you will be tempted to do otherwise. Sometimes, each of you will be tempted to go along with the crowd; other times, you'll be tempted to do things your way, not God's way. When you feel those temptations, resist them.

What will you allow to guide you through the coming day: your own desires (or, for that matter, the desires of your friends)? Or will you allow God to lead the way? The answer should be obvious. You should let God be your guide. When you entrust your life to Him completely and without reservation, God will give you the strength to meet any challenge, the courage to face any trial, and the wisdom to live in His righteousness. So trust Him today and seek His guidance. When you do, your next step will be the right one.

MORE THOUGHTS ABOUT GOD'S GUIDANCE

We must always invite Jesus to be the navigator of our plans, desires, wills, and emotions, for He is the way, the truth, and the life.

Bill Bright

It is a joy that God never abandons His children. He guides faithfully all who listen to His directions.

Corrie ten Boom

REMEMBER THIS

Would you like God's guidance? Then ask Him for it. When you pray for guidance, God will give it (Luke 11:9). So ask.

KEEPING A PROPER PERSPECTIVE THROUGHOUT THE SUMMER

Since you have been raised to new life with Christ,
set your sights on the realities of heaven,
where Christ sits at God's right hand in the place of
honor and power.

Colossians 3:1 NLT

Negative thoughts are habit-forming; thankfully, so are positive ones. With practice, you can form the habit of focusing on God's priorities and your own possibilities. When you do, you'll soon discover that you will spend less time fretting about your challenges and more time praising God for His gifts.

When you call upon the Lord and prayerfully seek His will, He will give you wisdom and perspective. When you make God's priorities your priorities, He will direct your steps and calm your fears. So today and every day hereafter, pray for a sense of balance and perspective. And remember: no problems are too big for God—and that includes yours.

MORE THOUGHTS ABOUT PERSPECTIVE

Instead of being frustrated and overwhelmed by all that is going on in our world, go to the Lord and ask Him to give you His eternal perspective.

Kay Arthur

Attitude is the mind's paintbrush; it can color any situation.

Barbara Johnson

A SUMMERTIME TIP

When you focus on the world, you lose perspective. When you focus on God's promises, you gain clearer perspective. So this summer, and every season hereafter, focus on God.

PRAISING GOD THROUGHOUT THE SUMMER

I will thank the Lord with all my heart;
I will declare all Your wonderful works.
I will rejoice and boast about You;
I will sing about Your name, Most High.

Psalm 9:1-2 Holman CSB

When is the best time to praise God? In church? Before dinner is served? When we tuck little children into bed? None of the above. The best time to praise God is all day, every day, to the greatest extent we can, with thanksgiving in our hearts.

Too many of us, even well-intentioned believers, tend to "compartmentalize" our waking hours into a few familiar categories: work, rest, play, family time, and worship. To do so is a mistake. Worship and praise should be woven into the fabric of everything we do; it should never be relegated to a weekly three-hour visit to church on Sunday morning.

Mrs. Charles E. Cowman, the author of the classic devotional text *Streams in the Desert*, wrote, "Two wings are necessary to lift our souls toward God: prayer and praise. Prayer asks. Praise accepts the answer." Today, find a little more time to lift your concerns to God in prayer, and praise Him for all that He has done. He's listening . . . and He wants to hear from you.

MORE THOUGHTS ABOUT PRAISE

Worship is an act which develops feelings for God, not a feeling for God which is expressed in an act of worship. When we obey the command to praise God in worship, our deep, essential need to be in relationship with God is nurtured.

Eugene Peterson

Be not afraid of saying too much in the praises of God; all the danger is of saying too little.

Matthew Henry

This is my story, this is my song, praising my Savior, all the day long.

Fanny Crosby

Words fail to express my love for this holy Book, my gratitude for its author, for His love and goodness. How shall I thank Him for it?

Lottie Moon

Nothing we do is more powerful or more life-changing than praising God.

Stormie Omartian

A SUMMERTIME TIP

If you want to make this the best summer ever, praise God more than you ever have before.

50

SHARING YOUR OPTIMISM THIS SUMMER

My cup runs over. Surely goodness and mercy shall
follow me all the days of my life;
and I will dwell in the house of the Lord Forever.
Psalm 23:5-6 NKJV

Christians have every reason to be optimistic about life. As John Calvin observed, "There is not one blade of grass, there is no color in this world that is not intended to make us rejoice." But, sometimes, rejoicing is the last thing on our minds. Sometimes, we fall prey to worry, frustration, anxiety, or sheer exhaustion, and our hearts become heavy. What's needed is plenty of rest, a large dose of perspective, and God's healing touch, but not necessarily in that order.

Today, why not claim the joy that is rightfully yours in Christ? Why not take time to celebrate God's glorious creation? Why not trust your hopes instead of your fears? When you do, you will think optimistically about yourself and your world . . . and you can then share your optimism with others. They'll be better for it, and so will you. But not necessarily in that order.

MORE THOUGHTS ABOUT OPTIMISM

The Christian lifestyle is not one of legalistic do's and don'ts, but one that is positive, attractive, and joyful.

Vonette Bright

REMEMBER THIS

Be a realistic optimist. Your attitude toward the future will help create your future. So think realistically about yourself and your situation while making a conscious effort to focus on hopes, not fears. When you do, you'll put the self-fulfilling prophecy to work for you.

PROBLEM-SOLVING 101

The righteous face many troubles, but the Lord rescues them from each and every one.
Psalm 34:19 NLT

Certainly, your family will experience its share of glitches this summer. After all, no season of life is completely problem-free.

The question is not whether we will encounter problems; the real question is how we will choose to address them. When it comes to solving the problems of everyday living, we often know precisely what needs to be done, but we may be slow in doing it—especially if what needs to be done is difficult. So we put off till tomorrow what should be done today.

The words of Psalm 34 remind us that the Lord solves problems for "people who do what is right." And usually, doing "what is right" means doing the uncomfortable work of confronting our problems sooner rather than later. So with no further ado, let the problem-solving begin . . . right now.

MORE THOUGHTS ABOUT
OVERCOMING PROBLEMS

Life will be made or broken at the place where we
meet and deal with obstacles.

E. Stanley Jones

Each problem is a God-appointed instructor.

Charles Swindoll

A SUMMERTIME TIP

This summer, think about the wisdom
of tackling your problems sooner rather
than later. Remember that "this, too,
will pass," but whatever "it" is will pass
more quickly if you spend more time
solving your problems and less time
fretting about them.

52

YOUR NOISY WORLD

Be silent before the Lord and wait expectantly for Him.
Psalm 37:7 Holman CSB

The world seems to grow louder day by day, and our senses seem to be invaded at every turn. But, if we allow the distractions of a clamorous society to separate us from God's peace, we do ourselves a profound disservice. Our task, as dutiful believers, is to carve out moments of silence in a world filled with noise.

If we are to maintain righteous minds and compassionate hearts, we must take time each day for prayer and for meditation. We must make ourselves still in the presence of our Creator. We must quiet our minds and our hearts so that we might sense God's will and His love.

Has the busy pace of life robbed you of the peace that God has promised? If so, it's time to reorder your priorities and your life. Nothing is more important than the time you spend with your Heavenly Father. So be still and claim the inner peace that is found in the silent moments you spend with God. His peace is offered freely; it has been paid for in full; it is yours for the asking. So ask. And then share.

MORE THOUGHTS ABOUT QUIET TIME

Jesus taught us by example to get out of the rat race and recharge our batteries.

Barbara Johnson

The manifold rewards of a serious, consistent prayer life demonstrate clearly that time with our Lord should be our first priority.

Shirley Dobson

A SUMMERTIME TIP

This summer, find time each day to be still and listen to God. He has something important to say to you.

OBSERVING THE SABBATH THROUGHOUT THE SUMMER... AND BEYOND

Remember the Sabbath day, to keep it holy.

Exodus 20:8 NKJV

When God gave Moses the Ten Commandments, it became perfectly clear that our Heavenly Father intends for us to make the Sabbath a holy day, a day for worship, for contemplation, for fellowship, and for rest. Yet we live in a seven-day-a-week world, a world that all too often treats Sunday as a regular workday.

How does your family observe the Lord's day? When church is over, do you treat Sunday like any other day of the week? If so, it's time to think long and hard about your family's schedule and your family's priorities.

Whenever we ignore God's commandments, we pay a price. So if you've been treating Sunday as just another day, it's time to break that habit. When Sunday rolls around, don't try to fill every spare moment. Take time to rest . . . Father's orders!

MORE THOUGHTS ABOUT THE SABBATH

God asks that we worship Him with our concentrated minds as well as with our wills and emotions. A divided and scattered mind is not effective.

Catherine Marshall

A SUMMERTIME TIP

This summer, think about new ways that you can honor God on the Sabbath. The Sabbath is unlike the other six days of the week, and it's up to you to treat it that way.

TODAY IS A TREASURE
FROM GOD

This is the day the Lord has made;
let us rejoice and be glad in it.
Psalm 118:24 Holman CSB

This day is a blessed gift from God. And as Christians, we have countless reasons to rejoice. Yet on some days, when the demands of life threaten to overwhelm us, we don't feel much like rejoicing. Instead of celebrating God's glorious creation, we may find ourselves frustrated by the obligations of today and worried by the uncertainties of tomorrow.

Every day should be a time for prayer and celebration as we consider the Good News of God's free gift: salvation through Jesus Christ. May we—as believers who have so much to celebrate—never fail to praise our Creator by rejoicing in His glorious handiwork.

So, whatever this day holds for your family, begin it and end it with God as your partner and

Christ as your Savior. And throughout the day, give thanks to the One who created you and saved you. God's love for you is infinite. Accept it joyfully . . . and be thankful.

MORE THOUGHTS ABOUT THE GIFT OF TODAY

When your life comes to a close, you will remember not days but moments. Treasure each one.

Barbara Johnson

Yesterday is the tomb of time, and tomorrow is the womb of time. Only now is yours.

R. G. Lee

If we are ever going to be or do anything for our Lord, now is the time.

Vance Havner

Wherever you are, be all there. Live to the hilt every situation you believe to be the will of God.

Jim Elliot

Love, joy, peace, patience, kindness, goodness, faithfulness, gentleness, and self-control. To these I commit my day. If I succeed, I will give thanks. If I fail, I will seek His grace. And then, when this day is done, I will place my head on my pillow and rest.

Max Lucado

SOMETHING TO THINK ABOUT

It's important to take time today to celebrate another day of life. And while you're at it, encourage your family and friends to join in the celebration.

USING YOUR GIFTS
THROUGHOUT
THE SUMMER

*I remind you to keep ablaze the gift of God
that is in you.*

2 Timothy 1:6 Holman CSB

God gives us talents for a reason: to use them. Each of us possesses special abilities, gifted by God, that can be nurtured carefully or ignored totally. Our challenge, of course, is to use our talents to the greatest extent possible. But we are mightily tempted to do otherwise. Why? Because converting raw talent into polished skill usually requires work, and lots of it. God's Word clearly instructs us to do the hard work of refining our talents for the glory of His kingdom and the service of His people.

The old saying is both familiar and true: "What we are is God's gift to us; what we become is our gift to God." May we always remember that our talents and abilities are priceless gifts from our Creator, and that the best way to say "thank you" for those gifts is to use them.

MORE THOUGHTS ABOUT USING OUR TALENTS

God often reveals His direction for our lives through the way He made us . . . with a certain personality and unique skills.

Bill Hybels

You are the only person on earth who can use your ability.

Zig Ziglar

Employ whatever God has entrusted you with, in doing good, all possible good, in every possible kind and degree.

John Wesley

God has given you special talents—now it's your turn to give them back to God.

Marie T. Freeman

If you want to reach your potential, you need to add a strong work ethic to your talent.

John Maxwell

You are a unique blend of talents, skills, and gifts, which makes you an indispensable member of the body of Christ.

Charles Stanley

REMEMBER THIS

Each person possesses special abilities that can be nurtured carefully or ignored totally. The challenge, of course, is to do the former and to avoid the latter.

56

TAKING TIME TO SAY "THANKS" THROUGHOUT THE SUMMER

Give thanks to the Lord, for He is good;
His faithful love endures forever.

Psalm 118:29 Holman CSB

As believing Christians, we are blessed beyond measure. God sent His only Son to die for our sins. And, God has given us the priceless gifts of eternal love and eternal life. We, in turn, are instructed to approach our Heavenly Father with reverence and thanksgiving. But sometimes, in the crush of everyday living, we simply don't stop long enough to pause and thank our Creator for the countless blessings He has bestowed upon us.

When we slow down and express our gratitude to the One who made us, we enrich our own lives and the lives of those around us. Thanksgiving should become a habit, a regular part of our daily routines. God has blessed us beyond measure, and we owe Him everything, including our eternal praise. To paraphrase the familiar children's blessing, "God is great, God is good, let us thank Him for . . . everything!"

MORE THOUGHTS ABOUT
SAYING "THANK YOU" TO GOD

The words "thank" and "think" come from the same root word. If we would think more, we would thank more.

Warren Wiersbe

God often keeps us on the path by guiding us through the counsel of friends and trusted spiritual advisors.

Bill Hybels

God is in control, and therefore in everything I can give thanks, not because of the situation, but because of the One who directs and rules over it.

Kay Arthur

It is always possible to be thankful for what is given rather than to complain about what is not given. One or the other becomes a habit of life.

Elisabeth Elliot

Do you know that if at birth I had been able to make one petition, it would have been that I should be born blind? Because, when I get to heaven, the first face that shall ever gladden my sight will be that of my Savior!

Fanny Crosby

SOMETHING TO THINK ABOUT

When is the best time to say "thanks" to God? Any time. God never takes a vacation, and He's always ready to hear from you. So what are you waiting for?

A RULE THAT'S GOLDEN

Just as you want others to do for you,
do the same for them.
Luke 6:31 Holman CSB

Life is simply better when we treat other people in the same way we would want to be treated if we were in their shoes. Things go better when we're courteous and compassionate. Graciousness, humility, and kindness are all virtues we should strive for. But sometimes, we fall short. Sometimes, amid the busyness and confusion of everyday life, we may neglect to share a kind word or a kind deed. This oversight hurts others, and it hurts us as well.

Today, slow yourself down and be alert for those who need your smile, your kind words, your hug, or your helping hand. Make kindness a centerpiece of your dealings with others. They will be blessed, and you will be, too. But not necessarily in that order.

MORE THOUGHTS ABOUT THE GOLDEN RULE

I have discovered that when I please Christ, I end up inadvertently serving others far more effectively.

Beth Moore

It is one of the most beautiful compensations of life that no one can sincerely try to help another without helping herself.

Barbara Johnson

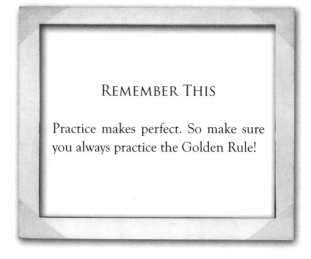

REMEMBER THIS

Practice makes perfect. So make sure you always practice the Golden Rule!

EVERY DAY WITH GOD

He awakens [Me] each morning;
He awakens My ear to listen like those being
instructed. The Lord God has opened My ear,
and I was not rebellious; I did not turn back.

Isaiah 50:4-5 Holman CSB

Summertime is a busy time, of course. But if you ever find that you're simply "too busy" for a daily chat with your Father in heaven, it's time to take a long, hard look at your priorities and your values. Each day has 1,440 minutes—do you value your relationship with God enough to spend a few of those minutes with Him? He deserves that much of your time and more—is He receiving it from you? Hopefully so.

As you consider your plans for the day ahead, here's a tip: organize your life around this simple principle: "God first." When you place your Creator where He belongs—at the very center of your day and your life—the rest of your priorities will fall into place.

MORE THOUGHTS ABOUT
SPENDING TIME WITH GOD

I suggest you discipline yourself to spend time daily in a systematic reading of God's Word. Make this "quiet time" a priority that nobody can change.

Dietrich Bonhoeffer

We must appropriate the tender mercy of God every day after conversion or problems quickly develop. We need His grace daily in order to live a righteous life.

Jim Cymbala

REMEMBER THIS

Never stop studying God's Word. Even if you've been studying the Bible for many years, you've still got lots to learn. Bible study should be a lifelong endeavor; make it your lifelong endeavor.

THE DIRECTION OF YOUR THOUGHTS

Finally brothers, whatever is true, whatever is honorable, whatever is just, whatever is pure, whatever is lovely, whatever is commendable— if there is any moral excellence and if there is any praise—dwell on these things.

Philippians 4:8 Holman CSB

Thoughts are intensely powerful things. Our thoughts have the power to lift us up or drag us down; they have the power to energize us or deplete us, to inspire us to greater accomplishments, or to make those accomplishments impossible.

How will you direct your thoughts today? Will you obey the words of Philippians 4:8 by dwelling upon those things that are honorable, true, and worthy of praise? Or will you allow your thoughts to be hijacked by the negativity that seems to dominate our troubled world?

Are you fearful, angry, bored, or worried? Are you so preoccupied with the concerns of this day that you fail to thank God for the promise of eternity? Are you confused, bitter, or pessimistic? If so, God wants to have a little talk with you.

God intends that you experience joy and abundance, but He will not force His joy upon you; you must claim it for yourself. It's up to you to celebrate the life that God has given you by focusing your mind upon "whatever is of good repute." Today, spend more time thinking about your blessings and less time fretting about your hardships. Then, take time to thank the Giver of all things good for gifts that are, in truth, far too numerous to count.

MORE THOUGHTS ABOUT THE POWER OF OUR THOUGHTS

The things we think are the things that feed our souls. If we think on pure and lovely things, we shall grow pure and lovely like them; and the converse is equally true.

Hannah Whitall Smith

It is the thoughts and intents of the heart that shape a person's life.

John Eldredge

People who do not develop and practice good thinking often find themselves at the mercy of their circumstances.

John Maxwell

Every major spiritual battle is in the mind.

Charles Stanley

REMEMBER THIS

Your thoughts have the power to lift you up or bring you down, so you should guard your thoughts very carefully.

THE GIFT OF
ETERNAL LIFE

For God loved the world in this way:
He gave His only Son, so that everyone who believes in
Him will not perish but have eternal life.
John 3:16 Holman CSB

Christ sacrificed His life on the cross so that we might have eternal life. This gift, freely given by God's only begotten Son, is the priceless possession of everyone who accepts Him as Lord and Savior. God is waiting patiently for each of us to accept the gift of eternal life. Let us claim Christ's gift today.

It is by God's grace that we have been saved, through faith. We are saved not because of our good deeds but because of our faith in Christ. May we, who have been given so much, praise our Savior for the gift of salvation, and may we share the joyous news of our Master's love and His grace.

MORE THOUGHTS ABOUT
ETERNAL LIFE

If you are a believer, your judgment will not determine your eternal destiny. Christ's finished work on Calvary was applied to you the moment you accepted Christ as Savior.

Beth Moore

The gift of God is eternal life, spiritual life, abundant life through faith in Jesus Christ, the Living Word of God.

Anne Graham Lotz

God did everything necessary to provide for our forgiveness by sacrificing His perfect, holy Son as the atoning substitute for our sins.

Franklin Graham

The damage done to us on this earth will never find its way into that safe city. We can relax, we can rest, and though some of us can hardly imagine it, we can prepare to feel safe and secure for all of eternity.

Bill Hybels

Teach us to set our hopes on heaven, to hold firmly to the promise of eternal life, so that we can withstand the struggles and storms of this world.

Max Lucado

The essence of salvation is an about-face from self-centeredness to God-centeredness.

Henry Blackaby

SOMETHING TO THINK ABOUT

God offers you life abundant and life eternal. If you have not accepted His gift, the appropriate moment to do so is now.